Bloom & Bones

by

Rae Howells & Jean James

First published 2021 by The Hedgehog Poetry Press,

5 Coppack House, Churchill Avenue, Clevedon. BS21 6QW

www.hedgehogpress.co.uk

ISBN: 978-1-913499-46-4

Contents

WHITE

Like your love, snow

is light, each flake made from a breath;
is porous, absorbing my voice;
is hard, a fist, a wedding-white death;
is heavy, pressing, stressing joists;

tells secrets, the heart-prints you left;
lies for you, too, covers your tracks;
holds, its cold an angel's caress;
thaws, its memory soft as wax.

This house

There are no carpets,
only floorboards painted white
worn bare in places where we used to walk.

Our animal tracks,
the trail we made now cold.
And in the jar, pebbles you found

stare back at me. I curl against
the chill you left, which, like your love,
is hard, a fist, a wedding-white death.

Animal tracks

Jonathon Donne is wanted for murder.
But he's been feeling easy,
skimming like a stone
up the early-hours tarmac,
weaselling along the foxlit road,
slipping between garages with peeling yellow doors.

Going loft to loft.
It's not the first time
he's followed the gold coins
of a fox's eyes into an alley,
bellied over a wall,
come to a battered back door
and buttered his way in.

Now he's spitting insulation,
tucked in strange eaves,
rockwool warm amongst somebody's boxed up books.
Itching. Thinking about the junk of his life,
thinking, thinking about the nylon rope,
the chemical fizz, his master,
the urine stink of his fear, the nicotine yellow of his teeth.
Wishing for a strong drag.

Outside in the gorse there's a glimpse of hi-vis.
Coppers, tracing a sparkling
trail of fibreglass,
following the acid gleam of his animal tracks.

Bitter lemons

Lily Driftwood in the Yellow House
is tucked into the eaves
remembering the bitter lemons of her life:

her bed the spattered floor,
a litter of tools, brushes and jars,
charcoals, pastels and paint.

Every morning she climbs into the canvas
to capture how the day comes filtering through shutters
onto the filigreed floor.

Today she's painting consolation:
an afternoon luminous with the gleam of goldfinches
upon the weedy fields.

At night when they tuck her in
she dreams amongst the branches
haloed in ochre light.

Yellow house is a colloquial expression in Russia for insane asylum.

ORANGE

Goldfinches

You're nine years old but even now, sometimes
you ask me to peel you an orange.
You watch, your cheeks clementine shiny, greedy
both for the fruit and my hands' knowledge,
envying, you say, the deft, capable way I unwrap it in tabs
the rind's eventual shape like a news channel world map.

You try to copy this method, thumbing your way in,
the flesh juicing beneath your grip.
Your world is a continental drift,
meridians untethered,
the pieces scattered.

We share the segments, taking turns.
I teach you to spit out the pips.
Your fingers are stained amber.
I wish I could keep you here, small, intact,
frozen in time, with that bitter-orange smell
lingering on our fingers.

It's not so long since you were taking shape in my rounded belly.
If only I could go back, to stand in the window
and watch the goldfinches,
their saffron wings ablaze,
teasing nyjer seed from the feeder,
easy in the air like hummingbirds.
            In my heaviness, I envied them.
I could feel the muscled goldfish of your body
turning on its axis inside my own,
the world spiralling out of you,
up and out of the sweet, swollen orange of my womb.

I remember eating a clementine, the juice sharp on my tongue.
Wondering if you could taste it too.

If you could taste it too

Georgia O'Keeffe tastes colours
rolls each one on her tongue like notes in music –
until a black door opens
into space
and a language without words
glows through.

In her hands' knowledge you can glimpse the possibilities –
the sharp of citrus bursting blood orange
from a canyon's crusted womb,
the swing of light illuminating
liminal hours.

She holds your gaze, painting a path
to faraway, asking you to be interested in the act of looking –
black and white, bloom and bones,
sun and shadow
and the landscape in between.

Bloom and bones

At Robin Hood's Bay, you stand on the village flagstones,
two girls blooming into the root and branch of yourselves like spring
blossom.
I'm high on your rose cheeks,
your fluorescent questions,
the chaffinch way you jostle and wing each other.

We take you down to the beach to show you how young you are.
                    Along the cliffline your grandfather shows you
how to crack open Cretaceous, Jurassic,
calcerous shales, mudstone, ironstone,
the skins of rock, once liquid,
that lipped and truffled ammonites, trilobites and shining black jet
into their silty mouths
and which now split apart, mud-pink, baring their broken teeth.

Your clever fingers are beaks picking through old bones.
The best finds go in the bucket.

On the way home, the treasure pail weighed between you,
we turn a wrong corner and come all at once upon a cherry tree
in full, glorious, flower, an unfolding, exploding, pink storm.
The first fruits are already growing,
swollen with stones, round and red as kisses.
You turn up your faces to blossom, and I see them,
the women in you, the leggy girls,
your laughing, easy fierceness, the ammonite curls of your shoulder blades
jostling out – the living bloom and bones of you.

You reach for cherries as petals drop around your shoulders,
pale, gorgeously silting up your fossil bucket.

Steersman

Buttressed in a theatre's jaws, the North Atlantic,
we listen as a man makes music,
clever fingers, beaks plucking through guitar strings.

A flamingo, long-shanked man playing flamenco,
patent shoes pinked in the footlights and
as he strums, the sea thrums to the swell.

Each rise and fall we follow on the heels of a storm,
travelling to a steersman's tunes, Scotland and Spain,
Ireland and Brazil, New Zealand and Crouch End –

his home, and us to ours, colours surfacing
chord after chord, a melody of places
couched in the chambers of the heart.

Storm

When air gets too hot, it flakes, turns itself brittle. And red.

So it was in 1976.
Summer had griddled on too long.
The suburbs became dense, vermillion
cul-de-sacs of melting tarmac.
The town's thighs were open and moaning for rain.
Our windless air became a block of cinnabar,
sweating out mercury,
the miraculous silver at its molten core
shimmering in the sky above roads.

You couldn't even ride your bike
on the molten wax of the pavements.
Each breath was hard won.
The people crying for their lost lawns couldn't make tears.
Grief was impossible:
the ground too hard for graves;
moles and badgers starved as worms slithered
down into the comparative cool of the underworld.
There was nobody left to eat the dead.

Then, one roaring morning, the red air juddered, solidified, sparked to life
as in a thunderstorm.
It was a miracle. A plague.
Oxygen and nitrogen crackled, clicked,
transfigured; sprouted hooked feet, antennae, elytra.

A billion ladybird larvae had come of age after 159 sultry, rainless days,
and now gorgeously swarmed every surface.
At the beach, the listless sea was enamelled scarlet.
Scorched yellow leaves turned hematite, bristling.
Poppies were resurrected. Aircraft disappeared into red clouds.
Roads crunched in a storm of brittle orange shells.
People fled from the bites of ladybirds as crazed with thirst
as everybody else.

Upstairs, we flung the window wide in hopes of rain.
The flaming sky kept going on, whitelessly.
We were overheated, wild. In drought measures. The radio said:
"Save water! Bath with a friend!"
Obediently we undressed, crackling out of shirts, shorts, underthings,
flexing the shining wings of our shoulderblades.

Meteoroids

My daughter lies flung out
against the stars,
incandescent,
shifting through space,
too soft for earth's hard crust.
She chose another path
leaving me trailing in her wake,
red-eyed,
treading on meteor dust,
squinting heavenward,
listening for the cry
that never came.

Because of Leonardo

In May when you lie sleeping with your naked feet coupled up together,
I can keep still and watch your glass heart tipping its breath into the violet evening,
and know – with all the kindly understanding of a surgeon – how grass seeds
might flow through its marvellous chambers to your mitral valve.

And when above you the moon's weightless smile looks down
and in the ghosted ball I see the old moon's archil face held tenderly
in the thin hands of the new, I can surmise Da Vinci's earthshine reaching up
from distant storm clouds to cross the dark space between us, to light the lunar night.

And when your breathing stutters and you dream you are a lion
moving through ancient streets towards the king, with your chest
stuffed full and bright with lilies, I can imagine the automatic cords and pulleys
of your limbs, the way your tongue makes its perfect movements,
the anatomical correctness of your proud jaw.

And when you wake and smile and explain how songbirds have both
a song and a call, the elaborate song they use for love, the call they keep for contact,
and how they open up their lovely throats as a cage of market-bought birds is flung open,
how the tailfeathers touched your lip as you slept, then we are suddenly together
on swan's mountain, building a flying machine of our own,
readying ourselves to leap into the next column of rising air.

But when I cut my goosefeather quill to a point of the very finest hair's width,
dip it in iron-gall ink and scratch these bruise-coloured marks on parchment,
I wonder - when five centuries of learning have passed - why nobody has yet explained
how the wild and farflung stars come to infiltrate the machinery of the human heart.

Inspired by The Five Faces of Leonardo, BBC Radio 4, first aired April and May 2019 on the 500th anniversary of the death of Leonardo Da Vinci.

Pond Skater

Over the land a purple curtain falls
with the weight of a thousand feathers, while
she sits,
in a wine-dark room made bright with lilies,
swallowing the silence.

Her eyes are bruises in the wolf moon's light.
A coil of amethysts bracelet her wrist as
she fumbles.
How strange that what seemed solid
now is molten,

a rippling surface for her pond skater beauty.
No gates can hold her,
she feels
the sluices open, sees the earth's curve,
a smile whose currents will carry her

out of the window on a violet tide,
past the banks pitted with blind-eyed burrows,
her final thought,
'How delicate the balance,'
before she tumbles.

BLUE

The banks

Shall we bless the bookkeepers, despairing over blue?
Their renaissance masters prized lapis lazuli,
the ice-blue rock mined, milled, mixed to
a precious paste, wrapped and brought along the silk road
from Sar-e-Sang to daub the artists' palettes of Europe.
How their patrons coveted ultramarine. A blue so blue it was *beyond sea,*
lasting, sparkling, keeping true to its blue heart.

Or shall we pity the bookkeepers, counting their masters' sovereigns,
forced to suffer the supply chain of divinity, sadness, modesty?
They paid more than gold for blue eyes, sapphire gowns, uncalm seas,
starry skies, the perfect Mary.
Shall we sigh for them, counting out ducats for an artist's pigment purchase,
demanding receipts, evidence of prudence
or drawing a grim line through item: *one pot of ultramarine,*
spilled in high-jinx by Rossetti, Morris and Byrne-Jones,
the short blue dash of a minus spoiling meticulous accounts?
Even their books were bound with blue, the sap of *hyacinthoides non-scripta:*
bluebell glue. Just think of the perfume of those ledgers.

By all means, but there's no need to sigh for me.
Outside my window, the woods are a painter's water jar,
the trees like brushes dipped in a glorious layer of paint-spoil,
a bluebell wash. Above, there is the indigo nib of a swift,
newly-arrived from Africa, barely touching the earth
as she wheels her careless zeroes on the sky's white page.
The slopes are a bluebell marketplace of delicate umbrella hooks
trading their grains of pollen; their scent rises.
How could I account for it? This blue is priceless, fleeting, *ultra.*

Because there, where my daughters run and play,
the banks, giving freely,
are proof that a life's work may be shaken out, enjoyed in a single season,
    that blue can be allowed to spill out or flutter by, uncounted,
    that in spring, time and beauty can – joyfully – be squandered,
    and will surely bloom again.

Out of the Blue

Once on feet of trilobites
we glided through earth's shallows.

Beneath the surface, snatching
at life, we grew a carapace over
slack skin, driving on relentlessly,
battering the shore
more and more,
until we forged a backbone

from no bone.

Slithering, undulating,
beyond sea,
we throbbed from deep,
refused to sleep,
fretting web-fingered,
drenched in slime, yet arrow-headed

out of the blue.

Our eyes popped
in the brilliance of the light,
our wild hearts pounded as
we charged down canyons,
scree-kneed, caped in otter skins,
tracks littering the landscape.

But we brought change,
pitched agony into oceans,
squandered the trees
stopped beaks with polymers.
Earth's scars are ours,
we carved them

in the stone.

Arrow heads

Out of a green sea,
arrow heads are knapped.
What splinting, what notching has happened here,
for wind to weaponise
birch?

Sometimes these canal-banks
spit out flints,
mudeyes goggling out –
an old hunter's living.
And in some other lights you can see bones sprout up from the earth;
ankles, wrists, ribs.

But the birchwood is no dusty museum cabinet of past wars, spent hunts.
The cold trunks are not skeleton.
An arrow can pierce the heart,
and birch shafts can thrust, love, lust.
On the hottest nights they thrill with sex,
fevered, ecstatic, overcome,
taking up a greenwood groan,
eyelids shimmering Verdigris,
legs wide, writhing to a deep beat.
Do you see it now? How the catkins are springs,
seed-engine coils,
sticky ovaries drooling on long twig-splits.
The jugular throb of sap rises,
opens, urging buds.

Upstairs in the dark rooms of the club,
chlorophyll drunk,
caterpillars fatten,
green veins gorged in absinthe light.
Soon they will be ready,
mothborn, fletched,
and the birch's taut bow
untensing
will fling them, heartlike, into flight.

Elsewhere

And suddenly you are back in the land of the Bogey Man,

the place you used to ramble as a child,
when you slipped out past the reassurance of cattle
clipping sweet grass at the bogland's edge.

In your outsize wellingtons you cross over the threshold
to the sponge of a fern bed cushioned among silver birches,
water-shanked, looming like swimmers out of a green sea.

You roam past waves in the ground, potato drills abandoned long ago.
Reeds sprout from your lips, and shards of the past sliver
through your tiny hands.

Your boots bore into ground and water, water and ground,
feet deep into memories of a blight in the soil,
a blight in the mind, and all the time in between

clutched in the bog's embrace, the place of the disappeared.

The Worm

There are days when nothing can be done
but taking to my wings

the wind is a road to the dragon's head,
the precious green trap
of horned rock snorting
in the sea's blue lung,

and I, a clay-brown kestrel,
softly, heartfully,
am a cello playing air
orchestral
vibrating
tucking in my wingbones
opening my bow to westerlies
sawing like a horse's tail against the Atlantic's cold reed

for both matinee and evening
the sea closes her lips
around the dragon's neck
stoppering the island's conduction to land
fluting
liquefying rock
water and ground

and lightly from the sand coloured cliffs,
my children like warm eggs in their semi-tone niches,
comes the deafening applause
of curtain down,
the thin causeway
unstringing

The Worm is what locals call the island of Worm's Head, Rhossili which is linked to the
headland by a causeway that is cut off every high tide. The name is thought to be a reference
to the island's dragon-like shape. .

Grounded

At Worm's Head
westerlies whip at
Helvetia's wreckage.

But let her lie,
wood bones Atlantic stripped,
tethered by sand.

Taken
so near her destination,
but the world

often
has other ideas,
sweeping us

off course,
shifting the journey
to a different shore.

Other ideas

& then one May morning we find a dead crow chick in the garden,
stubble-winged and hooded against its own death. Hardly

wrecked, as if trying to sleep through an operation by garlic-flower
surgeons and green nurses, quietly receiving the ministrations of flies,

which at first glance appear to be the anthracite stirrings of a heart above its chest,
a skittering hope, & yet like a curled, spent, leaf is how we find it, sleeping

carrion, unbreathing on the sprouting slope, blown somehow
off course, a young pink thing, almost comically bald, razored, & we wonder if,

the nest with its croaking parents – obscured but somewhere in the oaky silhouettes
high above us – is now empty. Later, when I turn out the light, the darkness is sudden

and profound, my pupils dilated to wormholes, and
startles up suddenly for the feather memory of my grandfather's

burnt hands in claws. He spent sentences on hospital wards. He wanted us to have
better days, away from the coalfields' casual snuffing out of life, the miner's lamp

on every sill like a stuttering lung. But maybe there is no such place of safety,
not even in the greenwild places. It's strange to think we watched the crows

rebuild their nest in spring, how we flushed to hear the luxurious clicks of their
lovemaking, only to find out that, all along, their plans were eggshells; & the world

had other ideas.

Blackthorn.

They called her the sullen tree,
bitter, spiny, shillelagh fodder,
home to the little folk,
waiting to do mischief
when our backs were turned.

They kept their distance,
left her proud right
in the middle of the back field,
barbed fence ringed to stop
the cattle coming close
and nudging her.

It was her powers
they feared,
pale skin, jet hair,
the yin and yang of
white blossom and black fruit,
too fierce a beauty.

We heard their stories
handed down
like sticks to beat us with,
a darkness sudden and profound,
obsidian
in waiting.

I never thought it.

Instead I studied how
light filtered through her thorns
down to the grass
that shifted at her feet
and sparked a hare
to rise up from its form.